Keto Ninja Foodi Cookbook #2019

Easy and Delicious Low Carb High Fat Ketogenic Recipes for a Healthy Keto Lifestyle (Burn Fat, Balance Hormones and Reverse Disease)

Gary Barnos

Table of contents

Introduction

Up until 2018 (the year of the Ninja Foodi), the Instant Pot was probably regarded as being the top of the game Electric Pressure Cooker in the market.

However, soon after the Ninja Foodi hit the market and people started to realize that this was undoubtedly one of the most, if the "THE" revolutionary electric pressure cooker of this generation, the appliance soon catapulted itself into stardom and will probably stay there as the next "King" for years to come.

We wholeheartedly appreciate the Instant Pot as it was one of the first appliances to bring together all of the common cooking appliances under one hood. The Instant Pot had the potential to be used as a sauté Pan, Steamer, Slow Cooker and so on.

But the Ninja Foodi keeps all of those functionalities, and takes things one step further by adding the features of an Air Fryer!

The auspiciously designed Ninja Foodi is probably the only appliance of its kind that combines the various functionalities of an Air Fryer, Slow Cooker and Instant Pot in a single appliance, and adds even more functions on top of all of them!

This amazingly made appliance acts as an all in one powerhouse that allows you to Air Fry, Pressure Cook, Steam, sauté etc. all using just a single kitchen appliance. This is truly a magnificent work of culinary art.

The Ninja Foodi comes with an amazingly designed "Crisping Lid" that allows the Ninja Foodi to seamlessly blend Air Frying with traditional pressure cooking. A dedicated pot known as the Crisping Basket is provided with the Ninja Foodi alongside a dedicated feature labeled "Air Crisp".

Since this book is about a Ketogenic Diet following the Ninja Foodi, the preliminary chapter of the book will cover the core ideas of the Ketogenic Diet itself, while the latter one will cover the basics of the Ninja Foodi.

After that, you will be greeted with a larger number of awesome recipes that will help you follow the Keto diet with ease and unleash the full potential of the Ninja Foodi!

Chapter 1: Understanding the Keto Diet

The History of Keto

The introduction pretty much gave you an idea of the Ketogenic Diet, so before going further, let me talk a little bit about the history of the Ketogenic Diet.

So, contrary to the belief of some people, the Keto diet isn't really a diet that just came out a few days back! In fact, the origin of the Ketogenic Diet has its root settled down back in the 1900s.

Unsurprisingly, that was also the time when a very large number of "Fad" diets started to pop up, all of which wanted to penetrate into the dietary market and get their share of consumers.

The Ketogenic Diet entered circulation in 1942 to be exact, which seemingly altered the whole dietary conception of every single individual at that time!

Dr. Russell is considered as the man behind this diet and is responsible for conceptualizing the concept of this diet. It is believed that he came up with the concept while working at the Mayo Clinic.

It should be kept in mind that though Russell's initial aim with this diet was not to solve dietary issues, rather, he wanted to find a diet that could help individuals who were suffering from Epilepsy,

Unsurprisingly, the Ketogenic Diet not only helped to cure epilepsy, but it seemed that it also significantly helped with weight loss as well!

After that discovery, the Ketogenic Diet got attention and reached the mainstream audience where it excelled in a market, saturated with hundreds of fad diets.

Just to clarify, the primary goal the Ketogenic Diet is to lower down your Carbohydrates intake and hence, lower down the over amount of Carbohydrates in your body. This will, in turn, lead your body into a state know n as "Ketosis" where the body starts to actually burn "Fat" instead of carbohydrates to produce energy for day to day activities.

The Process of Ketosis

When you are exposing yourself to a high-carb diet, you are constantly putting your body into a state of metabolic glycolysis where your body tries to get most of the energy required for day to day lives from blood glucose.

In this particular state, after each and every meal, your body experiences a spike in blood glucose levels that cause high levels of insulin to be released. This causes your body to store fatter and block the release of fat from your fat storages.

Alternatively, when you are on a low-carb and high-fat diet such as the Ketogenic diet pushes your body into a state of Ketosis. In this state, your body breaks down fat into "Ketone Bodies" (Ketones) and forces the body to use these Ketones as its primary source of energy.

While you are on Ketosis, your body will readily start to burn fat for energy and consume fat reserves to produce the daily required energy.

Whenever you are on low carbs for a few days, your body will start to adjust itself to the new form of diet and naturally kick-into ketosis.

Most cells in your body will start to use ketones and glucose for fuel and for the cells that can only take glucose, such as the parts of brain, glycerol derived from dietary fats is made into glucose by the liver through glucogenesis, which is then used by the brain.

The main goal of the Keto diet is to keep you in nutritional ketosis all the time! However, for those of you who are just starting on a Keto Diet, you need to be aware that it takes about 4-8 weeks for your body to fully adapt itself to Ketosis.

Once your body becomes Keto adapted though, glycogen will decrease and you will carry less water weight, your muscle endurance will increase and you will experience an overall increase in energy levels.

And not to mention:

- It will help you control your appetite
- It will improve your mental clarity
- It will lower down inflammation in your body

- It will improve the stability of your blood sugar levels
- It will eliminate the risk of heartburn
- It forces your body to burn fat as energy instead of carbs
- And most importantly, it does wonders for weight loss

Reaching Ketosis

While simply keeping your carb level under check will easily allow you to go into Ketosis, the following steps will also help you to reach Ketosis quickly and make it more effective:

- Keep your daily carbohydrate intake below 20g carbs
- Keep your protein levels at around 70g per day
- Don't starve! Swallow an adequate level of fat. Remember that the body is going to need fat to burn fat.
- Try to avoid snack times and stick to your breakfast, lunch and dinner meals with nothing in between.

As for how you are to understand that you are in Ketosis, the following are what you should know about:

- Your mouth will feel dry, and you feel have increased thirst
- The number of washroom visits will increase as you might need to urinate more often.
- Your breath will have a slight "Fruity" smell to it that will resemble that of a nail polish
- Aside from those three, you will obviously get the sensation mentioned above of having a low hunger level and increased bodily energy.

Benefits of Ketogenic Diet

If you follow a Ketogenic Diet properly, there are various health benefits (asides from slimming down) that you are going to experience in the long run! Some of the crucial ones are given below:

- ✓ The Ketogenic Diet will greatly help to lower down you're the "Bad" cholesterol in your body and improve the amount of healthy cholesterol, which will, in turn, help your cardiovascular system to a great extent
- ✓ Since the energy required by your body is produced by burning fat, your body will stay energized all throughout the day
- ✓ The fact that the Ketogenic Diet helps to lower down LDL level of your body, allows the diet to keep your protected against Type-2 Diabetes
- ✓ Following this Keto diet won't leave you hungry all throughout the day
- ✓ Asides from accelerating the fat burning process, Ketosis will also greatly enhance your skin condition by preventing various inflammation-related problems

As for the big "Cheese" of the diet as to the benefits of losing weight:

- The Keto Diet will help you gain greater control over your appetite and control the consumption of your food, this will easily contribute to losing more weight
- While you are on Ketosis, your body will start a process known as "Gluconeogenesis" that will further help to drop down your fat
- During your Ketogenic Diet, you are not only restricting your body from consuming large amounts of carbohydrates, but you are also preventing your body from consuming more calories, which contributes to weight loss as well
- While you are on a Ketogenic Diet, your body will be forced to ingest a large amount of protein, the increased consumption of protein will help you lose weight as well
- All things considered, following a proper Ketogenic diet is bound to greatly increase the amount of fat that is burnt through the day to day activities such. Not only that, but the increased ketones production will also contribute to burning an increasing amount of fat while exercising.

Keto-Friendly Tips

If you are a complete beginner, then following the Ketogenic Diet might be a little bit confusing for you! If that's the case, the following tips should help you to make your journey a lot smoother:

- Always make sure to keep drinking a good amount of liquids, you will be flushing away lots of electrolytes, it is advisable to replenish them in order to avoid side effects
- If you find yourself confused, try purchasing a nice carb counter to keep track of your carb intake
- It is essential that you try to include exercise into your daily routine in order to keep your body in tip-top shape
- Make sure to keep your sodium intake in check to avoid future problems during your Ketogenic journey. Easy steps may include
  - ✓ Drinking organic broth if possible
  - ✓ Taking a just a pinch of pink salt with you consumed meals
  - ✓ Adding about a ¼ teaspoon of pink salt to 16 ounces of water consumed
  - ✓ Adding vegetables such as kelp to your dishes
  - ✓ Eating up vegetables such as cucumber or celery for a more natural approach to sodium replenishment
- Before starting the journey, make sure to clean your pantry by getting rid of all high carb ingredients from your kitchen
- Try to follow the Ketogenic diet with a friend or another family member. It will help you stay encouraged and inspired all throughout the journey
- Make sure to eat a sufficient amount of food and maintaining the levels of fat, protein, and carbs as needed

Chapter 2: The Reinvention of Cooking Pot

What is Ninja Foodi?

The Ninja Foodi is possibly the most versatile and revolutionary kitchen appliance to date, and it has been pretty much "Reinventing" the wheel of Electric Pressure Cookers ever since it's conception.

The Ninja Foodi is essentially the only appliance in the market that has the capacity to work as an all in one device that offers a wide range of cooking functionalities including Slow Cooking, Sautéing, Pressure Cooking and even Air Frying!

This awesome and unique technology allows the user to seamlessly blend the functionalities of an Air Fryer and Pressure Cooker and create meals faster and more efficiently than any other appliance in comparison.

And just in case you are wondering, with this amazing device, you won't only be limited to simple pressure cooker dishes! The versatility of this appliance will allow you to create anything from soups, stews, chili's to breakfast and desserts! Your imagination is the only limitation here.

And at the heart of all these functionalities, is the groundbreaking technology that is known as the "TenderCrisp" tech.

What is TenderCrisp Technology?

Tendercrisp Technology stands at the heart of the Ninja Foodi cooking appliance that seemingly differentiates itself from the rest of the world. So, I strongly believe that it is really important that you have a good understanding of what this unique technology does.

So when you are pressure cooking tough ingredients such as meats, you end up with meals that are extremely juicy and satisfying to eat, but tender as well. Just pressure cooking alone won't be able to provide you with any crispy finish! This is where Air Frying comes in.

Air Frying utilizes the power of air to make foods crispier by giving it a nice tasty crust.

The revolutionary technology used in the Ninja Foodi allows a user to infuse both the effects of Pressure Cooking and Air Frying using just the single device! This basic cooking principle of combining both cooking methods is known as Ninja Foodie's proprietary TenderCrisp Technology.

In short, it allows you to create meals that are extremely tender and juicy on the side while having a satisfying crust on the surface.

The basic cooking procedure will ask you first to cook you a meal using pressure cooking, then use the Crisping Lid and Crisping Basket accompanied by the Air Crisp function to achieve your desired level of crispiness.

To better understand the mechanism at work here, the TenderCrisp technology utilizes superheated steam to infuse both flavors and moisture into your pressure-cooked food.

Afterward, the crisping lid blows extremely hot air to every side of your meal that gives it a fine golden color and crisp finish.

This unique combination is so far unachievable by any other appliance to date!

Benefits of Ninja Foodi

There is a wide array of benefits that you will enjoy while using the Ninja Foodi appliance, some of the core ones are given below:

Allows you to cook frozen food: Ninja Foodi will actually allow you to cook frozen food directly, saving a huge amount of time from your daily routine.

Let's you cook healthier meals: The precise cooking mechanism of the Ninja Foodi allows the appliance to preserve most of the nutrition of your meal while ensuring that your meals are undeniably delicious.

Acts as a one-stop shop: The versatility of the Ninja Foodi allows you to have a single appliance in your kitchen that does it all! Now you can keep your kitchen clean and pristine while cooking the meals that you love.

Allows cooking in a single pot: Single pot cooking is awesome! It's easy, efficient and creates a whole less mess. The flexibility of the Ninja Foodi allows you to prepare your meals

Frees up a lot of kitchen space: As mentioned in the previous point, since you have a single appliance that does pretty much that you could ask for, you will be freeing up lots of space in your kitchen!

Easy Cleaning: Cleaning the Ninja Foodi is extremely easy! Since all the cooking is done in a ceramic non-stick pot, just a little bit of soapy water is more than enough to keep the appliance clean.

Kills Any and All Harmful Micro-Organism: Sophisticated Electric Pressure Cookers such as the Ninja Foodi allows the internal temperature inside the pot to reach extremely high levels! This allows the pot to destroy most viruses and bacteria that might otherwise be harmful to your body. Some of the more resistant ones found in raw maize or corns can also be destroyed as well.

The Main Functions of Ninja Foodi

Just like other similar appliances, the wide array of options might seem a little bit daunting at first to new users.

The list below offers a brief look at all the functionalities of the core buttons that should help you understand what each of the main buttons does.

Pressure

Let's first talk about the single feature that you will be using most of the time. The Pressure function will allow you to use your Ninja Foodi as a Pressure Cooker appliance and cook your meals as you would in an electric pressure cooker such as the Instant Pot.

In this feature, foods are cooked at high temperature under pressure.

Just make sure to be careful when releasing the pressure! Otherwise, you might harm yourself.

There are essentially two ways through which you can release the pressure, which is discussed later on in the chapter.

Steam

Asides from Air Crisp, the Steam Function is probably one of the healthiest cooking options available in the Foodi!

The basic principle is as follows- Water is boiled inside the Ninja Foodi that generates a good amount of steam. This hot steam is then used to cook your ingredients kept in a steaming rack situated at the top of the inner chamber of your Pot.

Steaming is perfect for vegetables and other tender foods as it allows to preserve the nutrients while maintaining a nice crispy perfectly.

Asides from vegetables, however, the Steam function can also be used for cooking various fish and seafood, which are much more delicate than other red meats and chicken.

The process of steaming fish is the same, all you have to do is place them on the steaming rack.

Steaming the fish helps to preserve the flavor and moisture as well perfectly.

Slow Cooker

Despite popular belief, some foods tend to taste a whole lot better when Slowly Cooked over extremely low temperature for hours on end. This is why Slow Cookers such as the CrockPot are so popular amongst chefs and house makers!

The Slow Cooker feature of the Ninja Foodi allows you to achieve the same result, but without the need for a different appliance.

Ideal scenarios to use the Slow Cooker function would be when you want to cook your foods for longer to bring out the intense flavor of spices and herbs in stews, soups, and casseroles.

Since it takes a lot of time to Slow Cook, you should prepare and toss the ingredients early on before your feeding time.

For example. If you want to have your Slow Cooker meal for breakfast, prepare ingredients the night before and add them to your Foodi. The Foodi will do its magic and have the meal prepared by morning.

The Slow Cooker feature also comes with a HIGH or LOW setting that allows you to decide how long you want your meal to simmer.

Start/Stop Button

The function of this particular button is pretty straightforward; it allows you to initiate or stop the cooking process.

Sear/sauté

The Browning/sauté or Sear/sauté mode of the Ninja Foodi provides you with the means to brown your meat before cooking it using a just a little bit of oil. This is similar to when you are browning meat on a stovetop frying pan. And keeping that in mind, the Ninja Foodie's browning mode comes with five different Stove Top temperature settings that allow you to set your desired settings with ease.

Asides from browning meat, the different Stove Top temperatures also allows you to gently simmer your foods, cook or even sear them at very high temperatures.

Searing is yet another way to infuse the delicious flavors of your meat inside and give an extremely satisfying result.

This particular model is also excellent if you are in the mode for a quick Sautéed vegetable snack to go along with your main course.

Air Crisp

This is probably the feature that makes the Ninja Foodi so revolutionary and awesome to use! The Tendercrisp lid that comes as a part of the Ninja Foodi allows you to use the appliance as the perfect Air Fryer device.

Using the Tendercrisp lid and Air Crisp mode, the appliance will let you bake, roast, broil meals to perfection using just the power of superheated air! In the end, you will get perfectly caramelized, heartwarming dishes.

The Foodi comes with a dedicated crisping basket that is specifically designed for this purpose, which optimizes the way meals are air fried in the Foodi.

But the best part in all of these is probably the fact that using the Air Crisp feature, you will be able to cook your meals using almost none to minimal amount of oil!

It is also possible to combine both the pressure-cooking mechanism and Air Crisp function to create unique and flavorful dishes.

The Pressure-cooking phase will help you to seal the delicious juices of the meal inside the meat, while the crisping lid and Air Crisp mechanism will provide you to cook/roast your meal to perfection, giving a nice heartfelt crispy finish.

This combined method is also amazing when roasting whole chicken meat or roasts, as all the moisture remains intact and the final result turns out to be a dramatic crispy finish.

Bake/Roast

For anyone who loves to bake, this function is a dream come true! The Bake/Roast function allows the Foodi to be used as a traditional convection oven. This means you will be do anything that you might do with a general everyday oven! If you are in the mode to bake amazing cakes or casseroles, the Foodi has got you covered!

Broil

The main purpose of the Broil function is to allow you to use your appliance like an oven broiler and slightly brown the top of your dish if required. If you are in the mood for roasting a fine piece of pork loin to perfection or broiling your dish until the cheese melts and oozes, this mode is the perfect one to go with!

Dehydrate

In some more premium models of the Ninja Foodi appliance, you will notice a function labeled as "Dehydrate." This particular function is best suited for simple dried snacks such as dried apple slices, banana chips, jerky, etc. As you can probably guess, the core idea of this function is to suck out the moisture and dehydrate your ingredient into a hearty edible snack.

Chapter 3: Food to Eat and To Avoid

When following a Ketogenic Diet, following a proper food guide is crucial to the effectiveness of the diet. The following food list should help you understand the foods that you are allowed to go for and the ones that you should avoid.

Fats

Go For

- Saturated Fat like coconut oil ghee
- Monosaturated Fat like olive, macadamia, almond oil
- Polyunsaturated Omega 3s as sardines
- Medium Chain Triglycerides such as fatty acid
- Lard
- Chicken Fat
- Duck Fat
- Goose Fat

Not Go For

- Refined Fats and Oil as sunflower, soybean, corn oil, etc.
- Trans Fat such as margarine

Protein

Go For

- Grass-fed Meat
- Harvested seafood and wild caught meat
- Free-range organic egg
- Beef
- Lamb
- Goat
- Venison
- Pastured Pork
- Poultry

Not Go For

- Factory packed animal foods and produced

Vegetable

Go For

- Leafy green vegetables
- Low carb vegetables
- Swiss chard
- Bok Choy
- Lettuce
- Chard
- Chives
- Endives
- Radicchio

Not Go For

- High starchy= high carb vegetables such as peas, potatoes, yucca, beans, legumes.

Dairy Products

Go For

- Dairy products such as yogurt, sour cream, cottage cheese, goat cheese, and whole milk

Avoid

- Low fat/ Skimmed Milk etc.

Fruits

Go For

- In general, go for fruits that are on low carb and have more fat such as berries, avocados, etc.

Not Go For

- Try to avoid dried fruits that are high in sugar content

Drinks

Go For

- Water
- Black Coffee
- Unsweetened and Herbal Teas
- Nut Milk
- Light Beet
- Wine

Not Go For

- Drinks such as Pepsi or Coke
- High Fructose Syrup
- Nectar
- Honey
- Sodas

Sweets

Go For

- Stevia
- Xylitol
- Erythritol
- Inulin
- Monk Fruit Powder
- Cocoa Dark Chocolate

Chapter 4: Breakfast

Ingenious Cauliflower Hash Browns

Serving: **6**

Prep Time: **5 minutes**

Cook Time: **30-35 minutes**

Ingredients

- 6 whole eggs
- 4 cups cauliflower rice
- ¼ cup milk
- 1 onion, chopped
- 3 tablespoons butter
- 1 and ½ cups cooked ham, chopped
- ½ cup shredded cheese

Directions

1. Set your Ninja Foodi to sauté mode and add butter, let the butter heat up
2. Add onions and cook for 5 minutes until tender
3. Add iced cauliflower to pot and stir
4. Lock the Air Crisping lid and Air Crisp for 15 minutes, making sure to give them a turn about halfway through
5. Take a small bowl and mix in eggs and milk, pour mixture over browned cauliflower
6. Sprinkle ham over top
7. Press Air Crispy again and crisp for 10 minutes more
8. Sprinkle cheddar cheese on top and lock lid, let the crisp for 1 minute more until the cheese melts
9. Serve and enjoy!

Nutrition Values (Per Serving)

- Calories: 166

- Fat: 14g
- Carbohydrates: 3g
- Protein: 9g

Divine Vegetable Egg Casserole

Serving: **6**

Prep Time: **5 minutes**

Cook Time: **10 minutes**

Ingredients

- 4 whole eggs
- 1 tablespoons milk
- 1 cup ham, cooked and chopped
- ½ cup cheddar cheese, shredded
- ¼ teaspoon salt
- ¼ teaspoon ground black pepper

Directions

1. Take a baking pan (small enough to fit into your Ninja Foodi) bowl, and grease it well with butter
2. Take a medium bowl and whisk in eggs, milk, salt, pepper and add ham, cheese, and stir
3. Pour mixture into baking pan and lower the pan into your Ninja Foodi
4. Set your Ninja Foodi Air Crisp mode and Air Crisp for 325 degrees F for 7 minutes
5. Remove pan from eggs and enjoy!

Nutrition Values (Per Serving)

- Calories: 169
- Fat: 13g
- Carbohydrates: 1g
- Protein: 12g

Excellent Ham and eggs Casserole

Serving: **6**

Prep Time: **5 minutes**

Cook Time: **5 minutes**

Ingredients

- 4 whole eggs
- 1 tablespoons milk
- 1 tomato, diced
- ½ cup spinach
- ¼ teaspoon salt
- ¼ teaspoon ground black pepper

Directions

1. Take a baking pan (small enough to fit Ninja Foodi) and grease it with butter
2. Take a medium bowl and whisk in eggs, milk, salt, pepper, add veggies to the bowl and stir
3. Pour egg mixture into the baking pan and lower the pan into the Ninja Foodi
4. Close Air Crisping lid and Air Crisp for 325 degrees for 7 minutes
5. Remove the pan from eggs and enjoy hot!

Nutrition Values (Per Serving)

- Calories: 78
- Fat: 5g
- Carbohydrates: 1g
- Protein: 7g

Broccoli, Bacon and Cheddar Frittata

Serving: **4**

Prep Time: **5 minutes**

Cook Time: **10 minutes**

Ingredients

- 6 whole eggs
- 2 tablespoons milk
- ½ cup bacon, cooked and chopped
- 1 cup broccoli, cooked
- ½ cup shredded cheddar cheese
- ¼ teaspoon salt
- ¼ teaspoon ground black pepper

Directions

1. Take a baking pan (small enough to fit into your Ninja Foodi) bowl, and grease it well with butter

2. Take a medium sized bowl and add eggs, milk, salt, pepper, bacon, broccoli, and cheese

3. Stir well

4. Pour mixture into your prepared baking pan and lower pan into your Foodi, close Air Crisping lid

5. Air Crisp for 7 minutes at 375 degrees F

6. Remove pan and enjoy!

Nutrition Values (Per Serving)

- Calories: 269
- Fat: 20g
- Carbohydrates: 3g
- Protein: 19g

Early Morning Mushroom Soup

Serving: **4**

Prep Time: **10 minutes**

Cook Time: **10 minutes**

Ingredients

- 1 small onion, diced
- 8 ounces white button mushrooms, chopped
- 8 ounces portabella mushrooms
- 2 garlic cloves, minced
- ¼ cup dry white wine vinegar
- 2 and ½ cup mushroom stock
- 2 teaspoons salt
- 1 teaspoon fresh thyme
- ¼ teaspoon black pepper

Cashew Cream

- 1/3 cup of raw cashew
- ½ a cup of mushroom stock

Directions

1. Add onion, mushroom to the pot and set your Ninja Foodi to Sauté mode
2. Cook for 8 minutes and stir from time to time
3. Add garlic and Sauté for 2 minutes more
4. Add wine and Sauté until evaporated
5. Add thyme, pepper, salt, Mushroom stock, and stir
6. Lock up the lid and cook on HIGH pressure for 5 minutes
7. Perform quick release
8. Transfer cashew and water to the blender and blend well
9. Remove lid and transfer mix to the blender

10. Blend until smooth
11. Server and enjoy!

<u>Nutrition Values (Per Serving)</u>

- Calories: 193
- Fats: 12g
- Carbs:15g
- Protein: 5

Ginger and Butternut Bisque

Serving: **4**

Prep Time: **5 minutes**

Cook Time: **8 minutes**

Ingredients

- 1 cup of diced yellow onion
- 4 minced cloves of garlic
- 2 teaspoons of peeled and chopped ginger
- 1 cup of chopped carrot
- 1 green apple chopped
- 1 peeled and chopped butternut squash
- 1 teaspoon salt
- 2 cups of water
- ¼ cup of finely chopped parsley
- Black pepper

Directions

1. Prepare the ingredients accordingly and keep them on the side
2. Set your Ninja Foodie to Sauté mode and add onions, cook for minutes
3. Add just a splash of water
4. Add garlic, carrot, ginger, apple, squash, and salt
5. Give it a nice stir
6. Add water and lock up the lid
7. Cook on HIGH pressure for 5 minutes
8. Naturally, release the pressure
9. Allow it to cool for 15 minutes
10. Blend the soup in batches, or you may use an immersion blender as well to blend in the pot until it is creamy
11. Add parsley and season with some black pepper

12. Serve and enjoy!

Nutrition Values (Per Serving)

- Protein: 3g
- Carbs: 14g
- Fats: 5g
- Calories: 116

Early Morning Cauliflower Zoodles

Serving: **4**

Prep Time: **10 minutes**

Cook Time: **8 minutes**

Ingredients

- 2 tablespoons butter
- 2 cloves garlic
- 7-8 cauliflower florets
- 1 cup vegetable broth
- 2 teaspoons salt
- 2 cups spinach, coarsely chopped
- 2 green onions, chopped
- 1 pound of zoodles (Spiralized Zucchini)

Garnish

- Chopped sun-dried tomatoes
- Balsamic vinegar
- Gorgonzola cheese

Directions

1. Set your Ninja Foodi to Sauté mode and add butter, allow the butter to melt
2. Add garlic cloves and Sauté for 2 minutes
3. Add cauliflower, broth, salt and lock up the lid and cook on HIGH pressure for 6 minutes
4. Prepare the zoodles
5. Perform a naturally release over 10 minutes
6. Use an immersion blender to blend the mixture in the pot to a puree
7. Pour the sauce over the zoodles
8. Serve with a garnish of cheese, sun-dried tomatoes and a drizzle of balsamic vinegar

9. Enjoy!

<u>Nutrition Values (Per Serving)</u>

- Calories: 78
- Fats: 5g
- Carbs 0.6g
- Protein:8g

Chapter 5: Snacks and Appetizers

Juicy Pork Stuffed Jalapeno

Serving: **6**

Prep Time: **10 minutes**

Cook Time: **10 minutes**

Ingredients

- 2 pounds pork sausage, ground
- 2 cups parmesan cheese, shredded
- 2 pounds large sized jalapeno peppers sliced lengthwise and seeded
- 2 (8 ounces packages), cream cheese, softened
- 2 (8 ounces) bottles, ranch dressing

Directions

1. Take a bowl and add pork sausage, cream cheese, ranch dressing and mix well
2. Slice jalapeno in half, remove seeds and clean them
3. Stuff sliced jalapeno pieces with pork mixture
4. Place peppers in crisping basket and transfer basket to your Ninja Foodi
5. Lock Air Crisping lid and cook on Air Crisp mode for 10 minutes at 350 degrees F
6. Cook in batches if needed, serve and enjoy!

Nutrition Values (Per Serving)

- Calories: 609
- Fat: 50g
- Carbohydrates: 10g
- Protein: 29g

Feisty Zucchini Gratin

Serving: **4**

Prep Time: **10 minutes**

Cook Time: **15 minutes**

Ingredients

- 2 zucchinis
- 1 tablespoon fresh parsley, chopped
- 2 tablespoons bread crumbs
- 4 tablespoons parmesan cheese, grated
- 1 tablespoon vegetable oil
- Salt and pepper to taste

Directions

1. Pre-heat your Ninja Foodi to 300 degrees F for 3 minutes
2. Slice zucchini lengthwise to get about 8 equal sizes pieces
3. Arrange pieces in your Crisping Basket (skin side down)
4. Top each with parsley, bread crumbs, cheese, oil, salt, and pepper
5. Return basket Ninja Foodi basket and cook for 15 minutes at 360 degrees F
6. Once done, serve with sauce
7. Enjoy!

Nutrition Values (Per Serving)

- Calories: 481
- Fat: 11g
- Carbohydrates: 10g
- Protein: 7g

Mushrooms Appetizer with Sour Cream

Serving: **24**

Prep Time: **10 minutes**

Cook Time: **20 minutes**

Ingredients

- 24 mushrooms, caps and stems diced
- 1 cup cheddar cheese, shredded
- ½ orange bell pepper, diced
- ½ onion, diced
- 4 bacon slices, diced
- ½ cup sour cream

Directions

1. Set your Ninja Foodie to Sauté mode and add mushroom stems, onion, bacon, bell pepper and Sauté for 5 minutes

2. Add 1 cup cheese, sour cream and cook for 2 minutes more

3. Stuff mushrooms with cheese and vegetable mixture and top with cheddar cheese

4. Transfer them to your Crisping Basket and lock Air Crisping lid

5. Air Crisp for 8 minutes at 350 degrees F

6. Serve and enjoy!

Nutrition Values (Per Serving)

- Calories: 288
- Fat: 6g
- Carbohydrates: 3g
- Protein: 25g

Multi-Colored Brussels

Serving: **4**

Prep Time: **10 minutes**

Cook Time: **3 minutes**

Ingredients

- 1-pound Brussels sprouts
- ¼ cup pine nuts
- 1 tablespoon extra-virgin olive oil
- 1 pomegranate
- ½ teaspoon salt
- 1 pepper, grated

Directions

1. Remove outer leaves and trim the stems off the washed Brussels sprouts
2. Cut the largest ones in uniform halves
3. Add 1 cup of water to the Ninja Foodi
4. Place steamer basket and add sprouts in the basket
5. Lock up the lid and cook on HIGH pressure for 3 minutes
6. Release the pressure naturally
7. Transfer the sprouts to serving dish and dress with olive oil, pepper, and salt
8. Sprinkle toasted pine nuts and pomegranate seeds!
9. Serve warm and enjoy!

Nutrition (Per Serving)

- Calories: 118
- Fat: 10g
- Carbohydrates: 7g
- Protein: 3g

Lovely Chicken Stuffed Mushrooms

Serving: **12**

Prep Time: **10 minutes**

Cook Time: **15 minutes**

Ingredients

- 12 large fresh mushrooms, stems removed

Stuffing

- 1 cup chicken meat, cubed
- ½ pound, imitation crabmeat, flaked
- 2 cups butter
- Garlic powder to taste
- 2 garlic cloves, peeled and minced

Directions

1. Take a non-stick skillet and place it over medium heat, add butter and let it heat up
2. Stir in chicken and Sauté for 5 minutes
3. Add ingredients for stuffing and cook for 5 minutes
4. Remove heat and let the chicken cool down
5. Divide filling into mushroom caps
6. Place stuffed mushroom caps in your Crisping basket and transfer basket to Foodi
7. Lock Crisping Lid and Air Crisp for 10 minutes at 375 degrees F
8. Serve and enjoy!

Nutrition Values (Per Serving)

- Calories: 383
- Fat: 36g
- Carbohydrates: 4g
- Protein: 8g

Familiar Chicken Crescent Wraps

Serving: **4**

Prep Time: **15 minutes**

Cook Time: **15 minutes**

Ingredients

- 3 (10 ounces0 cans, almond flour crescent roll dough
- 6 tablespoons butter
- 2 cooked chicken breast, skinless boneless, cubed
- 3 tablespoons onion, chopped
- ¾ (8 ounces) package cream cheese
- 3 garlic cloves, peeled and minced

Directions

1. Take a skillet to place it over medium heat, add oil and let it heat up
2. Add onion and garlic ad Sauté until tender
3. Add chicken, cream cheese, butter, onion garlic to food processor and blend until smooth
4. Spread dough over a flat surface and slice into 12 equal sized rectangles
5. Spoon chicken blend at the center of each dough piece
6. Roll piece while wrapping inner filling completely
7. Place wrapped balls in Crisping basket
8. Insert basket to your ninja Foodi and lock Air Crisp Lid, Air Crisp for 15 minutes at 360 degrees F
9. Serve and enjoy!

Nutrition Values (Per Serving)

- Calories: 597
- Fat: 19g
- Carbohydrates: 5g

- Protein: 37g

Chapter 6: Vegetarian

Cheesy Cauliflower Delight

Serving: **6**

Prep Time: **10 minutes**

Cook Time: **35 minutes**

Ingredients

- 1 tablespoon Keto-Friendly mustard
- 1 head cauliflower
- 1 teaspoon avocado mayonnaise
- ½ cup parmesan cheese, grated
- ¼ cup butter, cut into small pieces

Directions

1. Set your Ninja Foodi to Sauté mode and add butter, let it melt
2. Add cauliflower and Sauté for 3 minutes
3. Add rest of the ingredients and lock lid, cook on HIGH pressure for 30 minutes
4. Release pressure naturally over 10 minutes
5. Serve and enjoy!

Nutrition Values (Per Serving)

- Calories: 155
- Fat: 13g
- Carbohydrates: 2g
- Protein: 7g

Amazing Spaghetti Squash Noodles

Serving: **4**

Prep Time: **5 minutes**

Cook Time: **7 minutes**

Ingredients

- 2 pound of spaghetti squash
- 1 cup of water

Directions

1. Take a paring knife and cut the spaghetti squash in half
2. Take a largely sized spoon and scoop out the center seeds and discard the gunk
3. Place the Ninja Foodi steamer insert inside the inner pot of your Ninja Foodi
4. Add 1 cup of water
5. Add the half-cut squashes to the steamer insert, making sure that the cut part if facing up
6. Lock up the lid and cook on HIGH pressure for 7 minutes
7. Once done, perform a quick release
8. Take the squash out and fork out the strings
9. Serve with sauce or your favorite topping!

Nutrition Values (Per Serving)

- Calories: 45
- Fats: 5g
- Carbs:7g
- Protein:3g

Garlic and Dill Carrot Fiesta

Serving: **4**

Prep Time: **10 minutes**

Cook Time: **10-15 minutes**

Ingredients

- 3 cups carrots, chopped
- 1 tablespoon melted butter
- ½ teaspoon garlic salt
- 1 tablespoon fresh dill, minced
- 1 cup of water

Directions

1. Add listed ingredients to Ninja Foodi
2. Stir and lock lid, cook on HIGH pressure for 10 minutes
3. Release pressure naturally over 10 minutes
4. Quick release pressure
5. Serve with topping of dill, enjoy

Nutrition Values (Per Serving)

- Calories: 207
- Fat: 16g
- Carbohydrates: 5g
- Protein: 8g

Spiced Up Cauliflower Steak

Serving: **4**

Prep Time: **5 minutes**

Cook Time: **4 minutes**

Ingredients

- 1 large head cauliflower
- 2 tablespoon extra-virgin olive oil
- 2 teaspoons paprika
- 2 teaspoon ground cumin
- ¾ teaspoon kosher salt
- 1 cup fresh cilantro, chopped
- 1 lemon, quartered

How To

1. Place the steamer rack into your Ninja Foodi
2. Add 1 and a ½ cups of water
3. Remove the leaves from the cauliflower and trim the core to ensure that it is able to sit flat
4. Carefully place it on the steam rack
5. Take a small bowl and add olive oil, cumin, paprika, salt
6. Drizzle the mixture over the cauliflower
7. Lock up the lid and cook on HIGH pressure for 4 minutes
8. Quick release the pressure
9. Lift the cauliflower to a cutting board and slice into 1-inch steaks
10. Divide the mixture among serving plates and sprinkle with cilantro
11. Serve and enjoy!

Nutrition Values (Per Serving)

- Calories: 283

- Fats: 19g
- Carbs: 18g
- Protein: 10g

Cool Caramelized Onion

Serving: **4**

Prep Time: **10 minutes**

Cook Time: **30-35 minutes**

Ingredients

- 2 tablespoons unsalted butter
- 3 large onions sliced
- 2 tablespoons water
- 1 teaspoon salt

Directions

1. Set your Ninja Foodi to Sauté mode and add set temperature to medium heat, pre-heat the inner pot for 5 minutes

2. Add butter and let it melt, add onions, water, and stir

3. Lock lid and cook on HIGH pressure for 30 minutes

4. Quick release the pressure

5. Remove lid and set the pot to sauté mode, let it sear in Medium-HIGH mode for 15 minutes until all liquid is gone

6. Serve and enjoy!

Nutrition Values (Per Serving)

- Calories: 110
- Fat: 6g
- Carbohydrates: 10g
- Protein: 2g

Hearty Special Lunch Worthy Green Beans

Serving: **4**

Prep Time: **5 minutes**

Cook Time: **5 minutes**

Ingredients

- 2-3 pounds fresh green beans
- 2 tablespoons butter
- 1 garlic clove, minced
- Salt and pepper to taste
- 1 and ½ cups of water

Directions

1. Add listed ingredients to Ninja Foodi
2. Lock lid and cook on HIGH pressure for 5 minutes
3. Quick release pressure

Nutrition Values (Per Serving)

- Calories: 87
- Fat: 6g
- Carbohydrates: 5g
- Protein: 3g

Cool Cauliflower Mash

Serving: **3**

Prep Time: **5 minutes**

Cook Time: **5 minutes**

Ingredients

- 1 tablespoon butter, soft
- ½ cup feta cheese
- Salt and pepper to taste
- 1 large head cauliflower, chopped into large pieces
- 1 garlic clove, minced
- 2 teaspoons fresh chives, minced

Directions

1. Add water to your Ninja Foodi and place steamer basket
2. Add cauliflower pieces and lock lid, cook on HIGH pressure for 5 minutes
3. Quick release pressure
4. Open the lid and use an immersion blender to mash the cauliflower
5. Blend until you have a nice consistency
6. Enjoy!

Nutrition Values (Per Serving)

- Calories: 124
- Fat: 10g
- Carbohydrates: 5g
- Protein: 5g

Spaghetti Squash Dipped in Sage Butter Sauce

Serving: 4

Prep Time: 5 minutes

Cook Time: 10 minutes

<u>Ingredients</u>

- 1 medium-sized spaghetti squash
- 1 and a ½ cup of water
- 1 bunch of fresh sage
- 3-4 garlic cloves, sliced
- 2 tablespoon of olive oil
- 1 teaspoon of salt
- 1/8 teaspoon of nutmeg

<u>How To</u>

1. Halve the squash and scoop out the seeds
2. Add water to your Ninja Foodi and lower down the squash with the squash halves facing up
3. Stack them on top of one another
4. Lock up the lid and cook on HIGH pressure for 3 minutes
5. Release the pressure over 10 minutes
6. Take a cold Sauté pan and add sage, garlic and olive oil and cook on LOW heat, making sure to stir and fry the sage leaves
7. Keep it on the side
8. Release the pressure naturally and tease the squash fibers out from the shell and plop them into the Sauté Pan
9. Stir well and sprinkle salt and nutmeg
10. Serve with a bit of cheese and enjoy!

<u>Nutrition (Per Serving)</u>

- Calories: 76
- Fat: 1g
- Carbohydrates: 14g
- Protein: 2g

Garlic and Ginger Red Cabbage

Serving: **6**

Prep Time: **5 minutes**

Cook Time: **8 minutes**

Ingredients

- 2 tablespoon coconut oil
- 1 tablespoon butter
- 3 garlic cloves, crushed
- 2 teaspoon fresh ginger, grated
- 8 cups red cabbage, shredded
- 1 teaspoon salt
- ½ a teaspoon pepper
- 1/3 cup water

Directions

1. Set your Ninja Foodi to Sauté mode and add coconut oil and butter, allow to heat up
2. Add garlic and ginger and mix
3. Add cabbage, pepper, salt, and water
4. Mix well and lock up the lid, cook on HIGH pressure for 5 minutes
5. Perform a quick release and mix
6. Serve and enjoy!

Nutrition Values (Per Serving)

- Calories: 96
- Fat: 6g
- Carbohydrates: 9g
- Protein: 1.8g

Homely Maple Glazed Carrots

Serving: **4**

Prep Time: **5 minutes**

Cook Time: **4 minutes**

Ingredients

- 2-pound carrot
- ¼ cup raisins
- Pepper as needed
- 1 cup of water
- 1 tablespoon butter
- 1 tablespoon sugar-free Keto friendly maple syrup

Directions

1. Wash, peel the skin and slice the carrots diagonally
2. Add the carrots, raisins, water to your Ninja Foodi
3. Lock up the lid and cook on HIGH pressure for 4 minutes
4. Perform a quick release
5. Strain the carrots
6. Add butter and maple syrup to the warm Ninja Foodi and mix well
7. Transfer the strained carrots back to the pot and stir to coat with maple sauce and butter
8. Serve with a bit of pepper
9. Enjoy!

Nutrition Values (Per Serving)

- Calories: 358
- Fats: 12g
- Carbs: 20g
- Protein: 1g

Chapter 7: Fish and Seafood

Delicious Panko Cod

Serving: **4**

Prep Time: **25 minutes**

Cook Time: **15 minutes**

Ingredients

- 2 uncooked cod fillets, 6 ounces each
- 3 teaspoons kosher salt
- ¾ cup panko bread crumbs
- 2 tablespoons butter, melted
- ¼ cup fresh parsley, minced
- 1 lemon. Zested and juiced

Directions

1. Pre-heat your Ninja Foodi at 390 degrees F and place Air Crisper basket inside
2. Season cod and salt
3. Take a bowl and add bread crumbs, parsley, lemon juice, zest, butter, and mix well
4. Coat fillets with the bread crumbs mixture and place fillets in your Air Crisping basket
5. Lock Air Crisping lid and cook on Air Crisp mode for 15 minutes at 360 degrees F
6. Serve and enjoy!

Nutrition Values (Per Serving)

- Calories: 554
- Fat: 24g
- Carbohydrates: 5g
- Protein: 37g

Delicious Paprika Salmon

Serving: **3**

Prep Time: **5 minutes**

Cook Time: **7 minutes**

Ingredients

- 2 wild caught salmon fillets, 1 to 1 and ½ inches thick
- 2 teaspoons avocado oil
- 2 teaspoons paprika
- Salt and pepper to taste
- Green herbs to garnish

Directions

1. Season salmon fillets with salt, pepper, paprika, and olive oil

2. Place Crisping basket in your Ninja Foodi, and pre-heat your Ninja Foodie at 390 degrees F

3. Place insert insider your Foodi and place the fillet in the insert, lock Air Crisping lid and cook for 7 minutes

4. Once done, serve the fish with herbs on top

5. Enjoy!

Nutrition Values (Per Serving)

- Calories: 249
- Fat: 11g
- Carbohydrates: 1.8g
- Protein: 35g

Warm Ranch Inspired Fillets

Serving: **3**

Prep Time: **5 minutes**

Cook Time: **13 minutes**

Ingredients

- ¼ cup panko
- ½ packet ranch dressing mix powder
- 1 and ¼ tablespoons vegetable oil
- 1 egg beaten
- 2 tilapia fillets
- A garnish of herbs and chilies

Directions

1. Pre-heat your Ninja Foodi with the Crisping Basket inside at 350 degrees F
2. Take a bowl and mix in ranch dressing and panko
3. Beat eggs in a shallow bowl and keep it on the side
4. Dip fillets in the eggs, then in the panko mix
5. Place fillets in your Ninja Foodie's insert and transfer insert to Ninja Foodi
6. Lock Air Crisping Lid and Air Crisp for 13 minutes at 350 degrees F
7. Garnish with chilies and herbs
8. Enjoy!

Nutrition Values (Per Serving)

- Calories: 301
- Fat: 12g
- Carbohydrates: 1.5g
- Protein: 28g

Lovely Swordfish

Serving: **3**

Prep Time: **5 minutes**

Cook Time: **150 minutes**

Ingredients

- 5 swordfish fillets
- ½ a cup of melted clarified butter
- 6 garlic cloves, chopped
- 1 tablespoon black pepper

Directions

1. Take a mixing bowl and add garlic, clarified butter, black pepper
2. Take a parchment paper and add the fillet
3. Cover and wrap the fish
4. Keep repeating until the fillets are wrapped up
5. Transfer wrapped fish to Ninja Foodi pot and lock lid
6. Allow them to cook for 2 and a ½ hour at high pressure
7. Release the pressure naturally
8. Serve and enjoy!

Nutrition Values (Per Serving)

- Calories: 379
- Fat: 26g
- Carbohydrates: 1g
- Protein: 34g

Fancy Mediterranean Cod

Serving: **4**

Prep Time: **10 minutes**

Cook Time: **15 minutes**

Ingredients

- 6 Fresh Cod
- 3 tablespoons clarified butter
- 1 lemon, juiced
- 1 onion, sliced
- 1 teaspoon salt
- ½ teaspoon pepper
- 1 teaspoon oregano
- 1 can (28 ounces) tomatoes, diced

Directions

1. Set your pot to sauté mode and add clarified butter
2. Once the butter is hot, add the rest of the ingredients and stir (except fish)
3. sauté for 10 minutes
4. Arrange the fish portions in the sauce and spoon the sauce over the fish to coat it
5. Lock up the lid and cook under HIGH pressure for 5 minutes
6. Perform a quick release and serve!

Nutrition Values (Per Serving)

- Calories: 301
- Fat: 14g
- Carbohydrates: 14g
- Protein: 47g

Beautiful Air Fried Scampi

Serving: **4**

Prep Time: **5 minutes**

Cook Time: **5 minutes**

Ingredients

- 4 tablespoons butter
- 1 tablespoon lemon juice
- 1 tablespoon garlic, minced
- 2 teaspoons red pepper flakes
- 1 tablespoon chives, chopped
- 1 tablespoon basil leaves, minced
- 2 tablespoons chicken stock
- 1-pound defrosted shrimp

Directions

1. Set your Foodi to sauté mode and add butter, let the butter melt and add red pepper flakes and garlic, sauté for 2 minutes
2. Transfer garlic to crisping basket, add remaining ingredients (including shrimp) to the basket
3. Return basket back to the Ninja Foodi and lock the Air Crisping lid, cook for 5 minutes at 390 degrees F
4. Once done, serve with a garnish of fresh basil

Nutrition Values (Per Serving)

- Calories: 372
- Fat: 11g
- Carbohydrates: 0.9g
- Protein: 63g

Loving Air Fried Scallops

Serving: **6**

Prep Time: **5 minutes**

Cook Time: **4 minutes**

Ingredients

- 12 scallops
- 3 tablespoons olive oil
- Salt and pepper to taste

Directions

1. Gently rub scallops with salt, pepper, and oil
2. Transfer to your Ninja Foodie's insert, and place the insert in your Foodi
3. Lock Air Crisping lid and cook for 4 minutes at 390 degrees F
4. Half through, make sure to give them a nice flip and keep cooking
5. Serve warm and enjoy!

Nutrition Values (Per Serving)

- Calories: 113
- Fat: 7.5g
- Carbohydrates: 1.4g
- Protein: 10g

Salmon with Lemon and Pepper

Serving: **3-4**

Prep Time: **5 minutes**

Cook Time: **6 minutes**

Ingredients

- ¾ cup of water
- Sprigs of parsley, basil, tarragon
- 1-pound salmon, skin on
- 3 teaspoons ghee
- ¾ teaspoon salt
- ½ teaspoon pepper
- ½ lemon, sliced
- 1 red bell pepper, julienned
- 1 carrot, julienned

How To

1. Set your Ninja Foodi to sauté mode and add water and herbs
2. Place a steamer rack and add the salmon
3. Drizzle ghee on top of the salmon
4. Season with pepper and salt
5. Cover lemon slices on top
6. Lock up the lid and cook on HIGH pressure for 3 minutes
7. Release the pressure naturally over 10 minutes
8. Transfer the salmon to a platter
9. Add veggies to your pot and set the pot to sauté mode
10. Cook for 1-2 minutes
11. Serve the cooked vegetables with salmon
12. Enjoy!

<u>Nutrition Values (Per Serving)</u>

- Calories: 464
- Fat: 34g
- Carbohydrates: 3g
- Protein: 34g

Tender Soft Salmon Fillets

Serving: **2**

Prep Time: **10 minutes**

Cook Time: **5 minutes**

Ingredients

- 2 salmon fillets
- ¼ cup onion, chopped
- 2 stalks green onion stalks, chopped
- 1 whole egg
- Almond meal as needed
- Salt and pepper to taste
- 2 tablespoons olive oil

How To

1. Add a cup of water to your Ninja Foodi and place a steamer rack on top
2. Place the fish
3. Season the fish with salt and pepper and lock up the lid
4. Cook on HIGH pressure for 3 minutes
5. Once done, quick release the pressure
6. Remove the fish and allow it to cool
7. Break the fillets into a bowl and add egg, yellow and green onions
8. Add ½ a cup of almond meal and mix with your hand
9. Divide the mixture into patties
10. Take a large skillet and place it over medium heat
11. Add oil and cook the patties
12. Enjoy!

Nutrition Values (Per Serving)

- Calories: 238

- Fat: 15g
- Carbohydrates: 1g
- Protein: 23g

Chapter 8: Poultry

Awesome Lemon and Chicken Delight

Serving: **2**

Prep Time: **10 minutes**

Cook Time: **18 minutes**

Ingredients

- 4 bone-in, skin on chicken thighs
- Salt and pepper to taste
- 2 tablespoons butter, divided
- 2 teaspoons garlic, minced
- ½ cup herbed chicken stock
- ½ cup heavy whip cream
- ½ a lemon, juiced

Directions

1. Season your chicken thighs generously with salt and pepper
2. Set your Foodi to sauté mode and add oil, let it heat up
3. Add thigh, Sauté both sides for 6 minutes
4. Remove thigh to a platter and keep it on the side
5. Add garlic, cook for 2 minutes
6. Whisk in chicken stock, heavy cream, lemon juice and gently stir
7. Bring the mix to a simmer and reintroduce chicken
8. Lock lid and cook for 10 minutes on HIGH pressure
9. Release pressure over 10 minutes
10. Serve and enjoy!

Nutrition Values (Per Serving)

- Calories: 294
- Fat: 26g
- Carbohydrates: 4g
- Protein: 12g

Homely Cabbage and Chicken Meatball

Serving: 2

Prep Time: 10 minutes + 30 minutes chill time

Cook Time: 4-6 minutes

Ingredients

- 1-pound ground chicken
- ¼ cup heavy whip cream
- 2 teaspoons salt
- ½ teaspoon ground caraway seeds
- 1 and ½ teaspoons fresh ground black pepper, divided
- 1/4 teaspoon ground allspice
- 4-6 cups green cabbage, thickly chopped
- ½ cup almond milk
- 2 tablespoons unsalted butter

Directions

1. Transfer meat to a bowl and add cream, 1 teaspoon salt, caraway, ½ teaspoon pepper, allspice and mix it well
2. Let the mixture chill for 30 minutes
3. Once the mixture is ready, use your hands to scoop the mixture into meatballs
4. Add half of your balls to Ninja Foodi pot and cover with half of the cabbage
5. Add remaining balls and cover with rest of the cabbage
6. Add milk, pats of butter, season with salt and pepper
7. Lock lid and cook on HIGH pressure for 4 minutes
8. Quick release pressure
9. Unlock lid and serve
10. Enjoy!

Nutrition Values (Per Serving)

- Calories: 294
- Fat: 26g
- Carbohydrates: 4g
- Protein: 12g

Hot and Spicy Paprika Chicken

Serving: **4**

Prep Time: **10 minutes**

Cook Time: **20-25 minutes**

Ingredients

- 4-piece (4 ounces each) chicken breast, skin on
- Salt and pepper to taste
- ½ cup sweet onion, chopped
- ½ cup heavy whip cream
- 2 teaspoons smoked paprika
- ½ cup sour cream
- 2 tablespoons fresh parsley, chopped

Directions

1. Season chicken with salt and pepper
2. Set your Foodi to sauté mode and add oil, let it heat up
3. Add chicken and sear both sides until nicely browned. Should take around 15 minutes
4. Remove chicken and transfer to a plate
5. Take a skillet and place it over medium heat, add onion and Sauté for 4 minutes
6. Stir in cream, paprika, bring the liquid to simmer
7. Return chicken to skillet and warm
8. Transfer the whole mixture to your Foodi and lock lid, cook on HIGH pressure for 5 minutes
9. Release pressure naturally over 10 minutes
10. Stir in cream, serve and enjoy!

Nutrition Values (Per Serving)

- Calories: 389

- Fat: 30g
- Carbohydrates: 4g
- Protein: 25g

Inspiring Turkey Cutlets

Serving: 4

Prep Time: 10 minutes + 30 minutes

Cook Time: 25 minutes

Ingredients

- 1 teaspoon Greek seasoning
- 1-pound turkey cutlets
- 2 tablespoons olive oil
- 1 teaspoon turmeric powder
- ½ cup almond flour

Directions

1. Take a bowl and add Greek seasoning, turmeric powder, almond flour, and mix
2. Dredge turkey cutlets in a bowl and let them sit for 30 minutes
3. Set Ninja Foodi to Sauté mode and add oil, let it heat up
4. Add cutlets and Sauté for 2 minutes
5. Lock lid and cook on LOW- MEDIUM pressure for 20 minutes
6. Release pressure naturally over 10 minutes
7. Take it out and serve, enjoy!

Nutrition Values (Per Serving)

- Calories: 340
- Fat: 19g
- Carbohydrates: 4g
- Protein: 36g

Fully Fluffed Up Whole Chicken

Serving: **6**

Prep Time: **10 minutes**

Cook Time: **8 hours**

Ingredients

- 1 cup mozzarella cheese
- 4 whole garlic cloves, peeled
- 1 whole chicken (2 pounds), cleaned and pat dried
- Salt and pepper to taste
- 2 tablespoons fresh lemon juice

Directions

1. Stuff chicken cavity with garlic cloves and mozzarella cheese
2. Season chicken generously with salt and pepper
3. Transfer chicken to Ninja Foodi and drizzle lemon juice
4. Lock lid and set to Slow Cooker mode, let it cook on LOW for 8 hours
5. Once done, serve and enjoy!

Nutrition Values (Per Serving)

- Calories: 309
- Fat: 12g
- Carbohydrates: 1.6g
- Protein: 45g

Butter and Garlic Foodi Chicken

Serving: **4**

Prep Time: **5 minutes**

Cook Time: **35 minutes**

Ingredients

- 4 pieces of chicken breasts chopped up
- ¼ cup of turmeric ghee/ normal ghee
- 1 teaspoon of salt
- 10 cloves of garlic, peeled and diced up

Directions

1. Add chicken breast to the Ninja Foodi
2. Add ghee, salt, diced garlic and lock up the lid
3. Cook on HIGH pressure for 35 minutes
4. Release the pressure naturally and open the lid
5. Serve with extra ghee

Nutrition Values (Per Serving)

- Protein: 47g
- Carbs: 3g
- Fats: 21g
- Calories: 404

Cool Duck Breast Meal

Serving: **2**

Prep Time: **120 minutes**

Cook Time: **30 minutes**

Ingredients

- 2 duck breast halves, boneless and skin on
- 1 teaspoon salt
- 2 teaspoons fresh garlic, minced
- ½ teaspoon black pepper
- 1/3 teaspoon thyme
- 1/3 teaspoon peppercorn
- 1 tablespoon olive oil
- 1 tablespoon apricot, peeled and cored
- 2 teaspoons date paste

Directions

1. Clean the duck breast and rub the spices all over
2. Cover and allow it to chill for 2 hours
3. Rinse the spices off and place the breast in a zip bag, seal it up making sure to remove as much air as possible. (look on the internet for immersion sealing method for best results)
4. Add 5 cups of water to your Ninja Foodi
5. Set your Ninja Foodi to sauté mode and allow the water to heat up for about 20 minutes
6. Place the bag in the water bath and keep it for 35-40 minutes
7. Remove the bag from water and pat the breasts dry
8. Sear the skin side of the duck breast in a nonstick frying pan with about 1 tablespoon of oil over medium-high heat
9. Turn the breast over and cook for 20 seconds more

10. Prepare the apricot sauce by mixing apricot and date paste in a small pot and bringing the mix to a boil, followed by a simmer for 5 minutes at low heat

11. Slice the duck breast and serve with apricot sauce

12. Serve the duck breast with the sauce

13. Enjoy!

<u>Nutrition Values (Per Serving)</u>

- Calories: 306
- Fats: 19g
- Carbs:8g
- Protein:17g

Garlic and Lemon Chicken Meal

Serving: **4**

Prep Time: **10 minutes**

Cook Time: **30 minutes**

Ingredients

- 2-3 pounds chicken breast
- 1 teaspoon salt
- 1 onion, diced
- 1 tablespoon ghee
- 5 garlic cloves, minced
- ½ cup organic chicken broth
- 1 teaspoon dried parsley
- 1 large lemon, juiced
- 3-4 teaspoon arrowroot flour

Directions

1. Set your pot to sauté mode
2. Add diced up onion and cooking fat
3. Allow the onions to cook for 5 -10 minutes
4. Add the rest of the ingredients except arrowroot flour
5. Lock up the lid and set the pot to poultry mode
6. Cook until the timer runs out
7. Allow the pressure to release naturally
8. Once done, remove ¼ cup of the sauce from the pot and add arrowroot to make a slurry
9. Add the slurry to the pot to make the gravy thick
10. Keep stirring well
11. Serve!

Nutrition Values (Per Serving)

- Calories: 462
- Fats: 60g
- Carbs:5g
- Protein:51g

Ham and Stuffed Generous Turkey Rolls

Serving: **4**

Prep Time: **10 minutes**

Cook Time: **20 minutes**

Ingredients

- 4 tablespoons fresh sage leaves
- 8 ham slices
- 8 (6 ounces) turkey cutlets
- Salt and pepper to taste
- 2 tablespoons butter, melted

Directions

1. Season turkey cutlets with salt and pepper
2. Roll turkey cutlets and wrap each of them with ham slices tightly
3. Coat each roll with butter and gently place sage leaves evenly over each cutlet
4. Transfer to Ninja Foodi
5. Lock lid and select Bake/Roast mode and bake for 10 minutes at 360 degrees F
6. Open lid and flip, lock lid and bake for 10 minutes more
7. Enjoy!

Nutrition Values (Per Serving)

- Calories: 497
- Fat: 24g
- Carbohydrates: 1.7g
- Protein: 56g

Chapter 9: Beef, Pork and Lamb

Tasty Beef Jerky

Serving: **6**

Prep Time: **10 minutes**

Cook Time: **20 minutes**

Ingredients

- ½ pound beef, sliced into 1/8-inch-thick strips
- ½ cup of soy sauce
- 2 tablespoons Worcestershire sauce
- 2 teaspoons ground black pepper
- 1 teaspoon onion powder
- ½ teaspoon garlic powder
- 1 teaspoon salt

Directions

1. Add listed ingredient to a large-sized Ziploc bag, seal it shut
2. Shake well, leave it in the fridge overnight
3. Lay strips on dehydrator trays, making sure not to overlap them
4. Lock Air Crisping Lid and set the temperature to 135 degrees F, cook for 7 hours
5. Store in airtight container, enjoy!

Nutrition Values (Per Serving)

- Calories: 62
- Fat: 7g
- Carbohydrates: 2g
- Protein: 9g

Homely Beef Stew

Serving: **4**

Prep Time: **10 minutes**

Cook Time: **10 minutes**

Ingredients

- 1-pound beef roast
- 4 cups beef broth
- 3 garlic cloves, chopped
- 1 carrot, chopped
- 2 celery stalks, chopped
- 2 tomatoes, chopped
- ½ white onion, chopped
- ¼ teaspoon salt
- 1/8 teaspoon ground black pepper

Directions

1. Add listed ingredients to your Ninja Foodi and lock lid, cook on HIGH pressure for 10 minutes
2. Quick release pressure
3. Open the lid and shred the bee using forks, serve and enjoy!

Nutrition Values (Per Serving)

- Calories: 211
- Fat: 7g
- Carbohydrates: 2g
- Protein: 10g

Cuban Garlic Pork Meal

Serving: **10**

Prep Time: **60 minutes**

Cook Time: **80 minutes**

Ingredients

- 3 pounds boneless pork shoulder blade roast, fat trimmed and removed
- 6 garlic cloves, minced
- 2/3 cup grapefruit juice
- ½ tablespoon fresh oregano
- ½ tablespoon cumin
- 1 lime, juiced
- 1 tablespoon salt
- 1 bay leaf
- Lime wedges as needed
- Cilantro, chopped, for garnish
- Hot sauce as needed
- Salsa as needed

How To

1. Cut the pork chops in 4 individual pieces and add them to a bowl
2. Take a small sized blender and add garlic, grapefruit juice, lime, oregano, cumin, salt, and blend well
3. Pour the marinade over your pork and allow it to sit for 60 minutes
4. Transfer the mix to your Ninja Foodi and add bay leaf
5. Cover and cook on HIGH pressure for 80 minutes
6. Release the pressure naturally
7. Remove the pork and shred it up
8. Return the pork back to the Foodi and add 1 cup of liquid
9. Season with some salt and allow it warm for a while (over sauté mode)

10. Enjoy!

<u>Nutrition Values (Per Serving)</u>

- Calories: 213
- Fat: 9g
- Carbohydrates: 2g
- Protein: 26g

The Original New York Strip Steak

Serving: **4**

Prep Time: **10 minutes**

Cook Time: **9 minutes**

Ingredients

- 24 ounces NY strip steak
- ½ teaspoon ground black pepper
- 1 teaspoon salt

Directions

1. Add steaks on a metal trivet and place trivet on your Ninja Foodi
2. Season with salt and pepper
3. Add 1 cup water to the pot (below steaks)
4. Lock lid and cook on HIGH pressure for 1 minute
5. Quick release pressure
6. Place Air Crisp lid and Air Crisp for 8 minutes for a medium-steak
7. Remove from pot and enjoy!

Nutrition Values (Per Serving)

- Calories: 503
- Fat: 46g
- Carbohydrates: 1g
- Protein: 46g

Butter and Dill Pork Chops

Serving: **4**

Prep Time: **5 minutes**

Cook Time: **20 minutes**

Ingredients

- 2 tablespoons unsalted butter
- 4 pieces ½ inch thick pork loin chops
- ½ teaspoon salt
- ½ teaspoon pepper
- 16 baby carrots
- ½ cup white wine vinegar
- ½ cup chicken broth

Directions

1. Set your Ninja Foodi to sauté mode
2. Season the chops with pepper and salt
3. Toss your chops into your pot and cook for 4 minutes
4. Transfer the chops to a plate and repeat to cook and brown the rest
5. Pour in 1 tablespoon of butter and Toss in your carrots, dill to the cooker and let it cook for about 1 minute
6. Pour in the wine and scrape off any browned bits in your cooker while the liquid comes to a boil
7. Stir in the broth
8. return the chops to your pot
9. Lock up the lid and let it cook for about 18 minutes at high pressure
10. Naturally, release the pressure by keeping it aside for 8 minutes
11. Unlock and serve with some sauce poured over

Nutrition Values (Per Serving)

- Calories: 296
- Fat: 25g
- Carbohydrates: 2g
- Protein: 17g

Premier Beef Roast

Serving: **4**

Prep Time: **10 minutes**

Cook Time: **43 minutes**

Ingredients

- 2 pounds chuck roast
- 1 tablespoon olive oil
- 1 teaspoon salt
- 1 teaspoon ground black pepper
- 1 teaspoon onion powder
- 1 teaspoon garlic powder
- 4 cups beef stock

Directions

1. Place roast in Ninja Food pot and season it well with salt and pepper
2. Add oil and set the pot to sauté mode, sear each side of roast for 3 minutes until slightly browned
3. Add beef broth, onion powder, garlic powder, and stir
4. Lock lid and cook on HIGH pressure for 40 minutes
5. Once the timer goes off, naturally release pressure over 10 minutes
6. Open the lid and serve hot
7. Enjoy!

Nutrition Values (Per Serving)

- Calories: 308
- Fat: 22g
- Carbohydrates: 2g
- Protein: 24g

Lemon-Y Pork Chops

Serving: **4**

Prep Time: **10 minutes**

Cook Time: **5 minutes**

Ingredients

- ½ cup hot sauce
- ½ cup of water
- 2 tablespoons butter
- 1/3 cup lemon juice
- 1-pound pork cutlets
- ½ teaspoon paprika

Directions

1. Add listed ingredients to your Ninja Foodi cook and crisp basket, place the basket inside

2. Lock lid and cook on HIGH pressure for 5 minutes, release pressure naturally over 10 minutes

3. Gently stir and serve, enjoy!

Nutrition Values (Per Serving)

- Calories: 414
- Fat: 21g
- Carbohydrates: 3g
- Protein: 50g

Boney Pork Chop Delight

Serving: **4**

Prep Time: **10 minutes**

Cook Time: **13 minutes**

Ingredients

- 4 and ¾ thick bone-in pork chops
- Salt and pepper as needed
- 1 cup baby carrots
- 1 onion, chopped
- 1 cup of mixed vegetables
- 3 tablespoons Worcestershire sauce

Directions

1. Take a bowl and add pork chops, season with pepper and salt
2. Take a skillet and place it over medium heat, add 2 teaspoons of butter and melt it
3. Toss the pork chops and brown them
4. Each side should take about 3-5 minutes
5. Set your Ninja Foodi to sauté mode and add 2 tablespoons of butter, add carrots and sauté them
6. Pour broth and Worcestershire
7. Add pork chops and lock up the lid
8. Cook on HIGH pressure for 13 minutes
9. Release the pressure naturally over 10 minutes
10. Enjoy!

Nutrition Values (Per Serving)

- Calories: 715
- Fat: 37.4g
- Carbohydrates: 2g

- Protein: 20.7g

Bacon and Brussels Delight

Serving: **4**

Prep Time: **10 minutes**

Cook Time: **5 minutes**

Ingredients

- 5 bacon slices, chopped
- 6 cups Brussels sprouts, chopped
- ¼ teaspoon salt
- Pepper as needed
- 2 tablespoons water
- 2 tablespoons balsamic vinegar

Directions

1. Set your Ninja Foodi to sauté mode and add chopped bacon, sauté until crispy
2. Add chopped Brussels sprouts and stir well to coat it
3. Add water and sprinkle a bit of salt
4. Lock up the lid and cook on HIGH pressure for 4-6 minutes
5. Release the pressure naturally
6. Set your pot to sauté mode and sauté the Brussels for a while longer
7. Transfer to serving the dish
8. Drizzle balsamic vinegar on top and enjoy!

Nutrition Values (Per Serving)

- Calories: 118
- Fats: 10g
- Carbs: 7g
- Protein: 3g

Lemon Pork Chops and Artichokes

Serving: **4**

Prep Time: **5 minutes**

Cook Time: **24 minutes**

Ingredients

- 2 tablespoons clarified butter
- 2 pieces 2-inch thick bone-in pork chops
- 3 ounces pancetta, diced
- 2 teaspoons ground black pepper
- 1 medium shallot, minced
- 4 lemon zest strips, 2-inch size
- 1 teaspoon dried rosemary
- 2 teaspoons garlic, minced
- 1 box (9 ounces) box frozen artichoke heart, quarters
- ¼ cup chicken broth

Directions

1. Set your pot to sauté mode and add pancetta, cook for 5 minutes
2. Transfer the browned pancetta to a plate and season your chops with pepper
3. Add the chops to your pot and cook for 4 minutes
4. Transfer the chops to a plate and keep repeating until they all of them are browned
5. Add shallots to the pot and cook for 1 minute
6. Add lemon zest, garlic, rosemary, and garlic, and stir until aromatic
7. After a while, stir in broth and artichokes
8. Return the pancetta back to the cooker
9. return the chops to your pot
10. Lock up the lid and let it cook for about 24 minutes at high pressure
11. Release pressure quickly
12. Unlock and transfer the chops to a carving board

13. Slice up the eye of your meat off the bone and slice the meat into strips
14. Divide in serving bowls and sauce ladled up

<u>Nutrition Values (Per Serving)</u>

- Calories: 286
- Fat: 26g
- Carbohydrates: 5g
- Protein: 10g

Chapter 10: Desserts

Hearty Vanilla Yogurt

Serving: 4

Prep Time: 10 minutes + 9 hours

Cook Time: 3 hours

Ingredients

- ½ cup full-fat milk
- ¼ cup yogurt started
- 1 cup heavy cream
- ½ tablespoon vanilla extract
- 2 teaspoons stevia

Directions

1. Add milk to your Ninja Foodi and stir in heavy cream, vanilla extract, stevia
2. Stir well, let the yogurt sit for a while
3. Lock lid and cook on SLOW COOKER mode for 3 hours
4. Take a small bowl and add 1 cup milk with the yogurt starter, bring this mixture to the pot
5. Lock lid and wrap Foodi in two small towels
6. Let it sit for 9 hours (to allow it to culture)
7. Refrigerate and serve
8. Enjoy!

Nutrition Values (Per Serving)

- Calories: 292
- Fat: 26g
- Carbohydrates: 8g

- Protein: 5g

Decadent Lemon Mousse

Serving: **2**

Prep Time: **10 minutes**

Cook Time: **12 minutes**

Ingredients

- 1-2 ounces cream cheese, soft
- ½ cup heavy cream
- 1/8 cup fresh lemon juice
- ½ teaspoon lemon liquid stevia
- 2 pinch salt

Directions

1. Take a bowl and mix in cream cheese, heavy cream, lemon juice, salt, and stevia

2. Pour mixture into a ramekin and transfer to Ninja Foodi

3. Lock lid and choose the Bake/Roast mode and bake for 12 minutes at 350 degrees F

4. Check using a toothpick if it comes out clean

5. Serve and enjoy!

Nutrition Values (Per Serving)

- Calories: 292
- Fat: 26g
- Carbohydrates: 8g
- Protein: 5g

Awesome Lemon Custard

Serving: **2**

Prep Time: **10 minutes**

Cook Time: **20 minutes**

Ingredients

- 5 egg yolks
- ¼ cup fresh squeezed lemon juice
- 1 tablespoon lemon zest
- 1 teaspoon pure vanilla extract
- 1/3 teaspoon liquid stevia
- 2 cups heavy cream
- 1 cup whipped coconut cream

Directions

1. Take a medium sized bowl and whisk in yolks, lemon juice, zest, vanilla, and liquid stevia
2. Whisk in heavy cream, divide the mixture between 4 ramekins
3. Place the included rack in your Ninja Foodi and place ramekins in the rack
4. Add just enough water to reach halfway to the sides of the ramekins
5. Lock lid and cook on HIGH pressure for 20 minutes
6. Release pressure naturally over 10 minutes
7. Remove ramekins and let them cool down
8. Chill in fridge, top with whipped coconut cream and enjoy!

Nutrition Values (Per Serving)

- Calories: 310
- Fat: 30g
- Carbohydrates: 3g
- Protein: 7g

Lovely Crème Brulee

Serving: **2**

Prep Time: **10 minutes**

Cook Time: **20 minutes**

Ingredients

- 1 cup heavy cream
- ½ tablespoon vanilla extract
- 3 egg yolks
- 1 pinch salt
- ¼ cup stevia

Directions

1. Take a bowl and mix in egg yolks, vanilla extract, salt, and heavy cream
2. Mix well and beat the mixture until combined well
3. Divide mixture between 4 greased ramekins and evenly transfer the ramekins to your Ninja Foodi
4. Lock lid and select the "Bake/Roast" mode, bake for 35 minutes at 365 degrees F
5. Remove ramekin from Ninja Foodi and wrap with plastic wrap
6. Refrigerate to chill for 3 hours
7. Serve and enjoy!

Nutrition Values (Per Serving)

- Calories: 260
- Fat: 22g
- Carbohydrates: 8g
- Protein: 5g

Wholesome Pot-De Crème

Serving: **4**

Prep Time: **10 minutes**

Cook Time: **20 minutes**

Ingredients

- 6 egg yolks
- 2 cups heavy whip cream
- 1/3 cup cocoa powder
- 1 tablespoon pure vanilla extract
- ½ teaspoon liquid stevia
- Whipped coconut cream for garnish
- Shaved dark chocolate for garnish

Directions

1. Take a medium sized bowl and whisk in yolks, heavy cream, cocoa powder, vanilla and stevia
2. Pour mixture in 1 and ½ quart baking dish, transfer to Nina Foodi insert
3. Add water to reach about half of the ramekin
4. Lock lid and cook on HIGH pressure for 12 minutes, quick release pressure
5. Remove baking dish from the insert and let it cool
6. Chill in fridge and serve with a garnish of coconut cream, shaved chocolate shavings
7. Enjoy!

Nutrition Values (Per Serving)

- Calories: 257
- Fat: 18g
- Carbohydrates: 3g
- Protein: 5g

Sweet Apple Infused Water

Serving: **4**

Prep Time: **2 minutes**

Cook Time: **4 minutes**

Ingredients

- 1 whole apple, chopped
- 5 sticks of cinnamon

Directions

1. Place the above-mentioned ingredients to a mesh steamer basket
2. Place the basket in your pot
3. Add water to barely cover the content
4. Lock up the lid and cook on HIGH pressure for 5 minutes
5. Once the cooking is done, quick release the pressure
6. Remove the steamer basket and discard the cooked produce
7. Allow the flavored water to cool and chill
8. Serve!

Nutrition Values (Per Serving)

- Calories: 194
- Fat: 0g
- Carbohydrates: 12g
- Protein: 0g

Warm Key Lime Curd

Serving: **4**

Prep Time: **10 minutes**

Cook Time: **10 minutes**

Ingredients

- 3 ounces unsalted butter
- 1 cup liquid stevia
- 2 large eggs
- 2 large egg yolks
- 2/3 cup fresh key lime juice
- 1-2 teaspoons key lime zest

Directions

1. Take food How Toor and add butter and stevia for 2 minutes
2. Slowly add the eggs and yolks to the processor and process to for 1 minute
3. Add Key Lime Juice to the blender and mix well
4. The mix should look curdled
5. Pour the mix into 3 one cup sized Mason Jars and lock up the lid
6. Place 1 and a ½ cups of water to your Ninja Foodi
7. Add the steamer basket/trivet
8. Place jars on the basket
9. Lock up the lid and cook for 10 minutes at HIGH pressure
10. Once done, allow the pressure to release naturally
11. Remove the jars and open the lids
12. Add Key Lime Zest to the curd and stir well
13. Place the lid and slightly tighten it
14. Cool for 20 minutes or chill in your fridge overnight
15. Enjoy!

Nutrition Values (Per Serving)

- Calories: 60
- Fat: 1g
- Carbohydrates: 11g
- Protein: 3g

Gallant Carrot Puree

Prep Time: **5 minutes**

Cooking Time: **4 minutes**

Serving: **4**

Ingredients

- 1 and a ½ pound of roughly chopped up carrots
- 1 tablespoon of butter at room temperature
- 1 tablespoon of agave nectar
- ¼ teaspoon of sea salt
- 1 cup of water

Directions

1. Clean and peel your carrots properly
2. Roughly chop up them into small pieces
3. Add 1 cup of water to your Pot
4. Place the carrots in a steamer basket and place the basket in the Ninja Foodi
5. Lock up the lid and cook on HIGH pressure for 4 minutes
6. Perform a quick release
7. Transfer the carrots to a deep bowl and use an immersion blender to blend the carrots
8. Add butter, nectar, salt, and puree
9. Taste the puree and season more if needed
10. Enjoy!

Nutrition Values (Per Serving)

- Calories: 143
- Fat: 9g
- Carbohydrates: 16g
- Protein: 2g

Clean and Simple Poached Pears

Serving: **6**

Prep Time: **5 minutes**

Cook Time: **10 minutes**

Ingredients

- 6 firm pears, peeled
- 1 bottle of dry red wine
- 1 bay leaf
- 4 garlic cloves, minced
- 1 stick cinnamon
- 1 fresh ginger, minced
- 1 and 1/3 cup stevia
- Mixed Italian herbs as needed

Directions

1. Peel the pears leaving the stems attached
2. Pour wine into your Ninja Foodi
3. Add bay leaf, cinnamon, cloves, ginger, stevia, and stir
4. Add pears to the pot and lock up the lid and cook on HIGH pressure for 9 minutes
5. Perform a quick release
6. Take the pears out using tong and keep them on the side
7. Set the pot to sauté mode and allow the mixture to reduce to half
8. Drizzle the mixture over the pears and enjoy!

Nutrition Values (Per Serving)

- Protein: 0.5g
- Carbs: 2g
- Fats: 16g
- Calories: 150

Conclusion

I would like to thank you again for purchasing the book and taking the time to go through the book as well.

I do hope that this book has been helpful and you found the information contained within the scriptures useful!

Keep in mind that you are not only limited to the recipes provided in this book! Just go ahead and keep on exploring until you find the Keto regime with the Ninja Foodi that works for you!

Stay healthy and stay safe!

44056918R00057

Made in the USA
Middletown, DE
02 May 2019